AMOUR

LET'S FALL IN LOVE

SANJANA

ISBN 979-888591338-6

Contents

Contents

Contents

"You are a poet's musing. When a poet writes you in their poetry, it's a blessing, but when you become their poetry, it's a miracle. A Poem is not just about words, rhymes, and patterns, it's about emotions and feelings a poet hides in between the lines."

About The Author

Sanjana is currently a student, and this is her debut book. She has been a co-author of various anthologies. She's a bibliophile and has a humongous collection of books. She aspires to become a professor and one of the bestselling authors in the future.

Instagram: floating._.emotions

Twitter: _sanjh_

Prologue

What happens when you fall in love?

The first thing that happens is you can't stop thinking about that one person. That one person becomes the centre of your life. Everything is suddenly about that one soul. You start creating scenarios in your head, you smile like an idiot. You start imagining things with that one person. People say love happens once, but it's not true. It happens many times. Until you get that one person worth every moment. Someone who deserves you, someone you deserve. Nothing really bothers you when you are with that one person. Nothing scares you, all you can see is his/her smile. All you want to do is to make that one-person smile. And you can do anything for him/her. Love heals you. Love reframes you. Love unleashes your true self, but with love comes fear. Fear of losing that person you love more than anything else. And that fear helps you fight every obstacle that comes in your way. You'll do anything to save your loved one. You'll put yourself at risk but won't let anything happen to him/her. This is how pure love is. This doesn't mean you'll always have happy moments, there will be times when you'll fight over stupid things.

Insecurities will build up... But all you need to do is support your partner. Have trust and faith in them. Communicate things. Understand each other. And then my friend you will have a life happier than ever before.

You'll feel the most precious and beautiful emotion. And at that moment you'll realize, what all happened was for a reason and was worth it. Every pain, every struggle, every drop of tear was worth it. Because now you have a smile, a smile so real that you can't justify its reality. This is what love is. This is what we live for. After all, what is life without love!

-Sanjana

Preface

AMOUR is a captivating book compiled with poetry about love, betrayal, and mixed emotions you feel when you fall in love. It has poems that can easily be connected with the realities of life. This book grips the emotions bled beautifully on the paper. It will take you on the journey of immense love, heartbreaks, and passion.

"There's a poet in you waiting to come out."

"AMOUR" will surely obsess you, possess you, and stay with you.

Acknowledgements

To my beloved Chosen Family,

Akshat without whose support and encouragement, I wouldn't have written this book. You have helped me so much. No words are enough to thank you.

Sakshi, never stopped inspiring me to write more and always had my back and gave me a push whenever I tried taking a step back. You never left my side and tolerated my being.

To my teachers, who believed in me.

To my family and friends, this wouldn't have been possible without your support.

1. Yearnings Of A Fragile Heart

Will you be my beginning?
Will you be my fresh start?
I know we are friends
But will you be my escape?
I'm not running away from reality
Don't get me wrong
But I want you to be my peace
My happy place..
My solace, my dead-end
My new beginning
No, we won't leave our lives behind
Things will stay where they belong
But can I know,
Where's my place
In your world..?
Am I a part of it?
Because tbh, you are becoming
The axis my world revolves on
But wait, am I asking for too much again?
Well, never mind, it'll only lead to more pain

2. A kind of Love

You know what's my kind of love?
I won't ask you out for fancy dates
I'll ask.. wanna lay under the night sky?
I won't ask you to attend super hyped concerts
I'd take you near a valley
we'd sit and listen closely
to the rustling leaves, and gorgeous waves
I won't surprise you with huge gifts
but I'd write poems
and cliche letters to you
I'd read you your favorite book
I'd hold your hand
in dark and in light
I'll hug you tight
after every fight
we won't carry grudges
through another night
I'll watch stars with you
I'll make hot coffee on a winter morning
and bring you ice creams at mid summer nights
I'll do whatever it takes to make you smile
for you, I'm ready to walk an extra mile

I'll prove my love with actions
and not just words
I'll love you right
I won't let love go out of your sight
if you please ..
I wanna make you mine

3. A Wish

Wish I wrote
Like I think..
Deeply, obsessively, desperately
With longings and desires
Setting souls on fire
I'd write about love
I'd write about hate
I'd write about romance
And things that are great
Even the things that aren't
And sunsets and rains
About sunrises and pain
I'd write about love without any gain
And more often, I'd write about you
And the memories you gave
I'd write about passion, aggression
And how warm your hugs feel
I'd write about the kiss I imagine
I'd portray my soul
In these words I hold
I'd write us
And emotions I behold.

4. Not your sunshine

I find you in sunsets
I find you in the stars
I find you in the core of my heart
You are there in my dreams,
Also present in my silent screams..
I can feel you around
And the emotions leave me to astound
I can imagine you
In my arms,
In my life,
In my future..
But I can't have you
Feels like.. it's against the law of nature
My heart was made with a broken mold
Yet, it has feelings,
That I tightly hold
My heart is just as brainless
As my brain is heartless
And I'm an old school
Hopeless romantic
Picturing you in an attic
With soft lights and hard floor

AMOUR

Welcoming us with an open door
But it's simply in my head
That I can make you mine
And fool of me to think
This could've been divine
But you like the moon
And I'm the sunshine..

5. To the person who'll love me someday

I love you
Terms and conditions apply
I love you,
But I won't share my room with you
I won't let you choose the color of curtains
They'll he red, forever
I love you,
I might ask you if u want a bite from my burger
But that's for the sake of manners
You aren't supposed to take it
I won't ever let you have the last slice of pizza
Else it'll turn into a war
I love you,
But I won't say it again and again
But I'll show it in little gestures I make
I won't let you sleep without eating
No, I'm not your mom
But I'll make sure you eat healthy
I won't let you work till late
I'll make delicious food for you

AMOUR

I'll cover you with blankets
On a cold night
And I'll add some of my love too
On a summer evening,
I'll bring you cold coffee
On a rainy day
I'll bring you a hot cup of tea
With tasty pakoras
And when you are feeling low
I'll be your high
I'll stay with you
And hug you tight
Until you feel alright..

6. A bridge

Of all the things I desperately want
I need a bridge from my heart to yours
a way so clear
all my thoughts and all my dreams
can reach you and stay near
oh love of mine
I want us to feel divine
Between like and love
There's a fine line
Which I wanna erase
And make you mine
As you got me thinking
If everything temporary
Feels permanent for a reason?
Or does this all depends
On our decision
But what is love without pain
And why do I expect any gain?
You are free to choose your way
Be it love
Or another memory lane…

7. In disguise

Before you love me
Let me warn you
Because my love might be different
From the people having hearts on their sleeves
I'd rather sit under the tree
And talk to its leaves
If you like roses
Just know it comes with thorns
And me, I have my demons too
I'm not a real happy person
But I assure you positive vibes
If you wanna feel loved
Come and talk to me at midnights
We'll make love with stars and the moon
Kisses are nice, cuddles too
But if you'd ask me
What I wanna do?
I'll take you to the roads not taken
And talk about life in outer planets
We'll go and sit on the rooftop
With deep conversations
A warm blanket in the sweater weather

A hot mug of coffee we'll hang together
I'd ask you to keep your head on my lap
If you're tired or feeling cold
I'll make it because
And you'll always have my arm to hold
If you fall in love with me
Just know your patience
As I'm not easy to handle
And my heart might be colder
Then the sweater weather.

8. If it's all part of a dream

I wanna hold your hand
I wanna kiss you slow
I wanna shed tears with you
And look at your afterglow
I wanna shower upon you
All my love and care
I wanna keep looking at you
I wanna keep you near
I wanna drown myself
In the depth of your eyes
I wanna reach places
Where happiness lies
I wanna lay my head
Right next to you
For hours and hours
I wanna talk to you
I wanna be there
When you are feeling low
I wanna stone you
With peace and happiness
I wanna make you feel high
I wanna take you to cloud 9

SANJANA

I wanna show you
How beautiful you are
But for me, this all is just a dream
Where reality is really far..
You are my friend
Close to my heart
I wanna keep this forever

9. In love with a sleepyhead

I am in love with a sleepyhead
Who sleeps while I talk
Who wakes up to my voice
Who fills my dark void
I am so in love with him
I wake up happy every morning
Waking up to wake him up
Sleeping to make him fall asleep
Thinking thoughts that are deep
Weaving dreams to feel him near
Telling him, he's mine without fear
Loving him with all the love I can
Every falling star I see
There's only one wish I make
To have you by my side
And make you stay for love's sake
They say , pain becomes art
But they don't know
Love creates art ...
I wanna hold you
Like a tree holds its last leaf
I wanna feel you

And the rhythm of your heart's beat
I wanna be the reason for your smile
Just the way you are mine...
If all this is in my head
If all this is just a dream
I wish the night never ends..
The dream never breaks...
And we stay like this... Forever

10. In afterlife

In the afterlife, I'll hold your hands
I'll kiss you in the streets
Knowing people are watching us
But there's nothing wrong
Maybe not now... But later
I'll love you to the core
Whenever you are ready for it
Our love will be the cure
For anything that's bothering
I'll dance with you under the rain
To our favourite song...
Washing away every pain..
Knowing..there's nothing wrong
Love is love
For whoever it's meant to be
You aren't just my crush...
But you are the one I love
because crushes are meant to break
But with you I'm whole...
And for this reason..
I'm ready to sacrifice my soul ...
Because you my love are the diamond in the mine of coal

11. Can love ever be a sin?

I'm falling in love all over again
But the feelings reside only in my heart
And it's okay if she wants to stay apart
I want her hands to hold mine
But she feels our friendship is divine
I wanna sin and swirl
But to her, this bond is holy and pure
I wanna hug her and hold her tight
What she wants is my biggest plight
I look at her with love and concern
She wants me to look away
I want her to feel my love...
But she has to run away.
My heart is at war
Losing every fight
I want her to be my love
But she wants to escape my sight.

12. Intimacy and cravings

The feeling of touch, skin to skin
Hands in hands, fingers entwined
Oh , the butterflies it gives
Imagine how divine it is
For you, it was just us holding hands
For me, it was a momentary illusion
Where I saw us happy
For those 12 seconds, I was on cloud 9'
Just like a happy child
My heart was racing wild
Beats getting faster
Still having a sense of calm
As crazy as it sounds
But you have that charm
The more I try to forget you,
The more you keep running in my mind
I wanna keep you close,
In the sacred corner of my heart
Yes you are the kind
One who never should stay apart
I'm falling for you more n more
But you can't pick me with love

I'm Dreaming about kissing you under the stars
Knowing the story behind every scar
I dream about you hugging me tight
And make me feel.. it's alright
But soon the reality checks in
Because for you, this all is nothing but a sin.

13. Love language

There you are,
Waiting for your perfect someone
The one they show in cliché romcoms
And here I'm waiting for your basic response
I might not have said those three words
But I expressed my love in various ways
Because I know, actions speak louder than words
Words you can ever say ....
My love was poured into the mug
When I made coffee, just the way you like
My love was mixed in the cake, I baked twice for you
And you said you loved it
I wish you'd love me too...
My love slipped into your hands
When we were crossing roads
Holding your hand , to keep you safe
No vehicle may harm you
Or cause you any bruise
I blowed my love in air
When I said the pizza is too hot
I fed you with my hands
Just to make sure...

You don't hurt yourself
As there wouldn't be any cure
And even now if you want me to say
How much I love you
In the old standard way
I'll say, it's raining outside
Don't forget your coat
You are too sensitive
Make sure you don't catch a cold.

14. The sky knows it all…

The sky knows
What I think at night
The moon knows
All that I wanted to say
All the conversation between us And moments that were right
Also the moments I wanted to create
All the things that you hate
And all the things you love
The stars are dancing To the rhythm of our song
A song you don't know of
A song is hidden in some corner of my heart
A song you might not be able to hear
because it needs to love my dear
I keep wishing
Worshiping the falling stars
For things to go well
For the love to bloom
How impossible can a wish be
To make sky turn black
Or wait, maybe
My love isn't pure enough
To win your love back

15. Moon knows you better

Laying down under the sky
I'm thinking of you..
So confused.. I don't know what to do..
I'm with him but I'm with you
When I peek inside my heart
I'm holding his hand
Still looking for you
I can't figure out
What's wrong with me..
Is it my overthinking..
Or my mind setting itself free
Looking for the missing pieces
Hidden under this mess
Will I lose me
Or will I lose you
Or will I lose him
Or am I losing us all together..
Am I falling in love with you
Or is this a sin..
because I'm thinking of you
Even when I'm with him...

16. A sight worth everything.

What a beautiful sight..
To watch you smile
When you are sleeping..
Wondering what you are dreaming…
Only if you could lay your head On my lap,
I'd shower you with love and care
I wanna caress your hair,
I wanna kiss you slow..
I wanna cheer you up
When you are feeling low..
I wanna love you right
I wanna hug you tight..
I wanna be your last thought every night..
But my feelings aren't your issues
I don't wanna trouble you
I don't wanna be the ache in your tissues..
I'll keep my love to myself..
You keep the friendship alive..
Maybe not now…
But we'll find love in the afterlife.

17. In order to save me

If I look away
While talking to you
Don't think I'm not interested
It's just me saving myself
from drowning in your ocean eyes
If I take your hands in mine
While crossing the road
Don't think of me as a perv
It's just my freak side taking care of you
Trying to keep you safe
If I talk about running away
When I'm still in love
It's me wanting to run towards you
But I don't wanna push your boundaries
It's just me, saving us from unwanted awkwardness
Keeping the Purity of our bond intact
With my love Leaving no impact.

18. Stay, just stay.

If I say I love you
I mean I love your soul
That too as a whole
You might be dumb
Or crazy too
But I'll stay near
No matter what you do
I know you and your worth
You aren't hopeless
Get this straight in your head
Your humor might be dead
But I'll never leave you on reading
When I say I will stay
I'll stay,
No matter what it takes
If you cry, I'll wipe your tears
If you're scared, I'll take away your fears
Commitment issues? We'll make it in a few years?
Feeling low? I know how to get you high
Wearing a frown? I'll remove every reason for your sigh..
Thinking about what I want in return??
Dumbo, just stay by my side..

19. Happy Place

You wanna stay at a happy place
And I wanna accompany you there
But I don't want you to fill my empty space
I wanna do it on my own my dear
I wanna be so complete And so bright
That I can brighten up even the city lights
And then , I wanna be the place
You were searching for
Happy and peaceful
Right now, I'm not in the right condition
But please don't abandon me
For I'm working on myself
Being better version of me
Keeping my feelings intact
Not just for your sake, But for mine too
Because if I wanna love you
I'll need to love myself too
More than ever before
And real than the reality
Fuck the similarity
And walk on foggy paths
Having eyes filled with clarity.

20. Forever is a dream?

I wonder why the feelings are so strong
And why am I so weak
My feelings won't go away
And I can't stay!
I want to stay
But I know you don't love me
I also wanna run away
But I'm holding into the hope
You'll love me.. if not today.. maybe someday
Someday when you fall
And I'll still be there to catch you
You'll come running to me
Breathless and yet kiss me
Hug me tight and it right
I still hope.. holding on will bring some plight
And it will be all
Worth every fight
Every war inside me
Between my heart and mind
Knowing you are one of a kind
And in your love
I'm being blind

Yet I see hope, yet I see you, yet I see us..
Together.. happy..
But still.. it's more of a dream..
just like 'FOREVER'

21. Listen, please?

Hey, listen closely to what I say
Oh wait.. you don't listen..
Okay.. at least read..
I love you..
Not only for your looks
But for soul
And when I say "you"
I mean it as a whole…
I love you and your twisted brain
Just like the initial of your name
I love you and your not so perfect legs
Your graceful confident walk
And also the way you talk
I love you for the way you blabber
About the most random thing
And the way you suffer in silence
Hiding your pain and the way it stings
I love you for the way your eyes shine
When you are floating on cloud nine
Also for the afterglow
For your oh so cute smile
I wish your lips could touch mine

I love your small hands
Beautiful fingers
The cake you bake
And the taste that lingers
I love you for your scars
And the stories they hide
I love you
For the way, you keep your chin up with pride
I love you for your sweet voice
Your melodious laughter
Non-stop blabbers
I love you now,
I'll love you forever
And also thereafter.

22. Cafune

I wanna hug you tight
I have basorexia
Cafune , my desire
My love, you are not lame
You are rame
You are that heavenly feeling
For which I always crave
I wanna count the stars with you by my side
I wanna see you smile
Hair behind your ears as I slide
I wanna see you blush
When I pull you close
And you get that adrenaline rush
I wanna be your comforter
When you're sad
I wanna be your high
When you're low
I wanna make you smile
After you're done crying
I wanna capture your afterglow
I wanna feel the feeling of love
I wanna feel the care you show

I wanna pamper you
I wanna spoil you with love and care
Breaking your heart, I won't dare
Where ever you go
Oh my love, I just wanna be there..

23. Can I believe you?

You say you don't love me
And I believe you
But I don't wanna learn this fact
I wanna undo the reality
Freaking out now and then
Still wanna hold to this virtuality
Imagining you by my side
Resting your head on my shoulder
Staying together, as we get older
Cuddling as the weather is now colder
Loving you, no matter where we go
Because now.. for you, I'm bolder
I'm scared to know the truth
As it hurts to see you without me
Pretending to live with glee
I wonder what's stopping you From loving me
Do you think I'll walk away?
Or are you not sure, Of me being enough
But oh dear love
I will fight for you and for us
I'll write for you, I'll grow for you
I'll do everything I can

I won't leave you behind
Make it worth every fight
I'll bring you light, I'll love you right
I'll stand for you
Even when I go weak in my knees
Just give me a chance
For your love, I plead.

24. Relax, but contraction??

I want my sufferings to end
I want my pain to fade
I want to see the sunrise
I'm tired of staying in the shade
But what would I write
If I have no pain
What will I admire
If I have no scars
How will I love
If I don't know how it feels
How will I sleep
Wondering what will I dream
How will I breathe amidst this suffocation
Stuck in an "oh so perfect life"
How will I live
If my muscles won't contract but only relax??

25. How are you?

"How are you?
I'm good.. you?"
How many feelings and emotions and truths are hidden
In between these two lines
When you ask.. how are you?
I wanna melt in ur arms, Cry my heart out
Tell you how much I fucking love you
How I feel when you are around
How much I cry at night
And everything u don't know about
How I notice everything u do
How I note ur likes n dislikes in my head
How nicely and neatly ..I've pasted your picture in my heart
And how heavy is the weight of my feelings
And how brutally it's tearing me apart
I wanna tell you about the dreams I weave
I wanna tell you
How much I crave for your hug which I never had
And may b I won't ever have
How fast my heart beats when u aren't around
And when u are there with me
How hard I try to keep you safe

AMOUR

Make you smile
And make every moment worth the while
I wanna tell you
Yours fears are right
But I'm worth the fight
Because I really wanna love you right
I wanna hug you tight
But all I say is, I'm fine
I'm good.. how are you?

26. Say you won't let go

I love you
From a distance..
Scared to get too close
And be lost
I love you
With my heart and soul
In love with you as a whole
You might not love me now
U might fall for me ever
But let me fall
Don't make me stop
Let me fall hard
And if I get hurt
Please, just be there
With ointment in your hand
And care in your heart.

27. Mission love

I'm risking so much loving you
But when our souls meet..
I wonder is it worth it?
Duh.. of course, it is
Running after you
Holding you close
Walking together on the path we chose
Munching and jumping like maniacs
But who cares
We aren't minions
Crying on your shoulder
And pulling you close.. as the air now feels colder
Babe, I'm a hoarder
Remembering dates and keeping the moments safe
Capturing them in heart
Having them locked away
Honey .. please stay..
I know you will, But I like to say
If I showed you my flaws
If I couldn't be strong
I know.. for sure
You will love me the same

Because we are happy together
And we get each other
There is so much left in us
Even eternity will fall short
But this mission is love..
I will never abort!

28. Can I see you??

you say you can't love
you say you can't be mine
Let's keep it simple..
and make this divine
fuck all the Mr. and Miss right
just enjoy this little ride??
I know you're scared of all this love drama
But we can still be crazy no baba??
I'll sit by the side
Somewhere between the nature
I'll be clingy
But I won't ask you for a forever
I'll rest my head on your shoulder
I'll hold you close
When the weather is colder
I'll keep you close
No matter what path you chose
I'll keep you near
But I won't burden you with I love yous'
Or borahaes
Or other cliché stuff
But I'll still share lovey-dovey posts

And defend you when you are being roast
I'll walk on the traffic side
Holding your hand so you don't stumble .alryt?
When it rains.. I'll hold an umbrella
When it's sunny
I'll be your shade
I'll cook.. according to your taste
We'll go slow.. very slow
Because with you.. I don't need any haste
As the meet
And as we talk
As we look at each other
I always want the time to stop
I wanna spend hours and days
and weeks and years with you
But I'll stay only as long as you want me to
I'll keep loving you
But I won't really tell
Maybe my actions will make it up for it
But I'll keep it simple
I'll just stay by your side
Staring at you
Admiring this heavenly sight!

29. I wanna love you right

I don't wanna romance you
But I wanna love you
I wanna be there by your side
And hold you uptight
When your world falls apart
I wanna caress your head
And pat your back
When you achieve even a small milestone
On your path I wanna be there
When you cry
I wanna wipe yours tears
I wanna stay by your side
Even at midnight
When you are sick
I wanna massage your head Relax your body and mind
I wanna stick by you, Through thick and thin
I wanna turn your frown into a grin
I don't wanna romance you
But I really really wanna love you
Love you to the extent, That you forget
What sense of fright looks like
I really really wanna make you feel alright.

30. Can I hold you again?

I'm going back to the places
Where we went together
Sitting on the wooden plank
But not resting my head on your shoulder
Letting the waves kiss my feet
But not running around you near the shore
I still go to our favorite spot.. alone
Admiring nature.. feeling the breeze
I still visit the restaurants
Where we ate together
Where..even the staff started to recognize us
They come to my table.. asking
Is your friend coming??
I simply say no with a smile
Hiding.. how painful that question seems
I still go to the holy places we visited
Saving "Prasada" for you
Only to realize later
You won't be there to have it..
I still go to our favorite ice cream parlor
Eating your favorite flavour
But nothing feels the same

AMOUR

It all has a different vibe now
The dosa isn't tasty anymore
The Prasada isn't that peaceful
No amount of ice cream is enough to curb my craving
No amount of warmth makes me feel because
Sometimes all I need is your hug
Sometimes all I can think about is you
But I can't even look at your pictures without shedding tears
These all are growing my fears
I'm scared to be lonely
Yet I'm all alone
I need you here
But it seems like.. you are long gone.

31. When I'm all alone.

I NEVER believed in miracles
Until I met YOU
You were everything, I ever wished for
Somethings are needed to end
For better things to begin
There is so much love in friendship
And so less friendship in love
But can love survive without friendship?
Or can love even have its existence ??
Without your love
I felt as if I'm living alone
But in a carnival
Everything around was cheerful
Except for my life
But without your friendship …
Like 100 ant bit me
And my feet turned cold
It was just as painful, And again..
I'm back into my broken mold
But in the end..
I learned .. how strong I can be
When I'm all alone.

32. In my dream.

In my dream world
We are happy together
We live in the same room
Feeling safe in each other's arm
Having dumb conversations
Sharing oversized clothes
Cuddling through the cold nights
Smuggling chill beers and Maggie at 3a.m.
You come n hug me tight
After that nasty fight
Kissing good mornings
Making breakfast together
Sharing secrets and also our lives
Adjusting through the situations
Staying close
Walking together on the path we chose
Side by side
Hand in hand
From 'I' to 'us'
'Mine' to 'ours'
Filling the walls with pictures
Capturing moments

Even though we suck at poses
Playing stupid games
and kissing the one who loses
yeah we're smart
and yes.. here.. in my dream..
we never drift apart.

33. Love, I'm home

Love ...I'm home
I say as I reach for the door
closing behind everything
that keeps you away from me
as i come home
to my home, which is you
i wanna look into your eyes
and read your day
I wanna listen to your essay
on how your day was
and what all you did
and everything about you
so nothing is kept hidden
I wanna share little things that happen
I wanna live every moment with you
wishing this lasts forever
I wanna keep holding your hands
until we are old
and our hair turns grey
I wanna hold on the to moments
as on your lap, I lay
making plans for a lazy Sunday

SANJANA

I wanna ease your soul
I wanna love you as a whole
I wanna be the one
who'll massage your head
with warm oil and warmth of love
to relax your body and calm your soul
I wanna be there
to wrap you with becauseiness
when the weather turns cold
I don't know how..
but I wanna be your love
and make you my home.

34. It's you, always

People always ask..
Why you?? Why not someone else??
How do I tell them..
You are the earth to my moon
You are the sun to my earth
How do I say
I don't need reasons
To fall for you my love
But if you wanna know
I'll share a few
I fell for the curve of your lips
I fell for the way you walk
I fell for the way you talk
I fell for the scars you wear
I fell for the way you keep me near
And I'm still falling
Harder day by day
Imagining you by side
I'm sleeping in the warmth of love
I'm feeling safe
I'm feeling like I'm home again
And all this was worth every pain

SANJANA

I wish to express my love
I wish to hug to tight
I wish to share this poem
When the time is right
When the time is right

35. Downhill

When I fell in love with you
My life became colorful
You were the long lost color to my life
I've always lived in a black and white world
Where darkness was my only friend
And then you stumbled into my life
Now I can't let go of your hand
We were doing great
Then suddenly everything went downhill
I couldn't get over the fact you were gone
I can't imagine going back to a life where you can't be mine
I needed you so bad by my side
But you weren't there and
my life was again black and white

36. Love can only be felt

I know the feeling of love
Love with no strings attached
Love is hidden in a box
Box filled with memories
Box filled with years of friendship
I've seen love from so close
I could touch it, I could sense it
I could see it, I could feel it
Love, borrowing pen and never returning it
Keeping it close as it contains her essence
Love keeping even the dead flowers
As they have her touch
Love, having a gallery filled with pictures
Pictures of her
Love, writing poems on love
Love, miraculously expressing feelings to her
Love, giving her silly names
Love, having her soul intact
Love, imaging scenarios in head
Love, being silly
Not caring if it's bad
Love filled with love

AMOUR

And purest of pure emotions
Love laying head on her lap
love, being a friend
love, being love
love, being there .. till the very end

37. If you see…

If I could lend you my eyes
I'd show you heavenly is your sight
You took me back to the time
When I was whole
And my heart was intact
I'd show how it feels
To feel suddenly alive
And it's not so hard to survive
I swear that every word I write
And every song I sing
I feel you around
I imagine you with me
I carried weight of unhappiness
You took it off and brought in life
Life so colorful and cheery
I started feeling so alive
I craved for something I had no clue about
And then you were here by my side
And now everything feels so divine
I wish I could show you
How you look in my sight.

38. You are my poetry

When I write about you
I imagine your soul in my poems
Your heart in the rhythm
Your fragrance in the pages
You are present in between the lines
In hidden emotions
Everlasting inspiration
You are the moon in my nights
The stars , shining bright
You are my sunshine
Bestowing upon me rays of hope and life
You are the colors to my rainbow
cloud to my raindrops
You are the deepest desire I hold in my heart
You are there in my dreams
In the scenes I imagine
You are my daily dose of happiness
You, darling, are my love
You are the reason of my being
And you are a part of my soul
You, my love, are my poem, My musings
And all the feelings I behold.

39. You are my home

I walked through the door with you
But something about it felt like home
My heart and mind are now like a place
Where freely you roam
All I wonder about is you
All I ever think about is you
You are there in my dreams
You are there in my imaginations
Fantasies so real and divine, It makes my soul revive
My fingers running through your hair
Your fragrance lingers even in my bones
As I close my eyes and lay my head
Your lap is the most becauseiest place
Even though the surroundings are too dark
Your shiny eyes bring out the spark
Lightening up my gloomy life
Exchanging my Monday blues with weekend vibes
I'm so intensely worshiping you
Scared to open my eyes, As this all is still a dream
I see with my open eyes
You are the home
Where my peace lies..

40. Another weekend??

I remember loving you
I remember holding you
I remember smiling with you
Holding your huge hands with little of mine
Roaming around, going places no one ever would
Finding peace in togetherness
Chaos in the lone time
I remember picking out vegies
And putting in your mouth
And you forcing me to eat broccoli
That taste still lingers
But the only tasty thing was your fingers
Haha, kidding, u smell like mayo
I remember fighting for the last bite
Of everything we ate
And how brutally you ignored my puppy face
Maggie hotdog burger pizza
Everything is losing its charm
I'm miserable, don't know how to stay calm
I'm pushing you away
But I need you near
I'm just a messed up girl

SANJANA

I need you to hear
But it's better to give up
As holding on hurts
Just like every story
Ours came to an end
May b it's a season
And we'll see each other
On some other weekend

41. Soulmates are not always lovers

Being in love is one selfless act
An act so real, it overpowers reality
Staying in love is even scary
As true love demands nothing but happiness
The happiness of the beloved
At first, I thought
True love has no existence
But I was so wrong
It does exist, like a pure soul
Real and rare
Beautiful like Kohinoor
But still has no greed
Selfless like saint
In front of whom
Every leisure fails…
I found one such rare soul
And his heart is made of gold
He gives everything
But expects nothing
He's there when I need him

He's there when I want him
He's there, even when I push him away
He's there always
Giving meaning to forever
His love is so pure and gentle
His touch is so divine
Giving up everything, considering himself as mine
His love never died
From my best to my worst
He kept all the strings tied
So far we have a bond so special
We think of the same things
We are different humans
But our souls are connected
We aren't lovers, sad for me
But we are soulmates
Not that I don't love him
But the way he does..
I'm far away
I'm scared, yet I hold him tight
We stay together, even after a brutal fight
We are one,Even when we aren't
We are real, We are whole
We are incomplete with each other's soul
Whoever says love doesn't exist
Just meet him
And you'll fall in love with love itself.

42. On the roadside

I dream of dreams I once dreamt
I cry the tears never wept
Us standing in the lake hugging each other
While the tiny waves kissed our feet
Slowly you were moving away
While there I was, standing still
I wanted to hug you for long
But as I opened my eyes
You were gone
I went deeper into the lake
Expecting you to come
And hold me back
But to think of anything..
The senses you lack
I wanted you near
You were drifting apart
I could feel myself
Losing pieces of my aching heart
But you going through the same
Hiding tears under the rain
Our hearts going insane
Not able to carry this unbearable pain

But holding on won't hurt this time
Trust me, our friendship is like old wine
Unaware of what the future holds..
Let's just leave it on the roads..

43. We'll meet again

We'll meet again
When we are whole and untorn
This is not a goodbye,
This will not last forever
We'll meet again
When the time is right
When we'll hold each other tight
This won't tear us apart
We'll meet again
Until then, there will be no more late-night talkings
Before we lay our heads to sleep
No more shoulder to lean on
When we need to cry and weep
This won't make us weak
We'll meet again
But before that,
Can we hold each other one last time
Can we love each other
And pretend it's alright
Can we whisper those three words
We long to hear
Tell me you love me

Just the way I do
Tell me you need me
Just the way we used to
We'll meet again
Until then,
Can we hold on to the memories we made
Can we have one more moment,
Before it's too late..

44. 116 Moons

116 moons, yet I wanna look into your eyes.
Thank you for the happiest time of my life
Maybe we can get better people,
But what matters is what we want...
What we need
We don't need more or less love
We need our love,
We need the one we love,
And not love the one we need..
Love needs to be unconditional
And without any greed
The same old fashioned love
Is what we really need
The one where we could cuddle all night
The one where we could fall for every sight
The one where we could hug each other tight
The one where everything feels alright!!!
With you, i have this feeling
It's not just two hearts dealing
It's two souls being entwined
With their scars revealing!!

The same old fashioned love
Is what we have
What we want
And what we need!!

45. You made me believe in soulmates

I don't believe in soulmates
But "since the day I met you
I met myself,
You were like a candle in my darkroom
You are blessing
I asked from the falling stars
If my heart could speak,
It would say
I won't let you go,
I wanna be with you forever
And also thereafter
Not even an eternity
Will be enough to be with you
Meeting you was my destiny
And keeping you is my choice
Having a friend like you
Is in itself a rejoice
I can be cliché
I can be lame
But I'm the vibe

You won't get again"
So be my soulmate
Stay with me
I promise to turn your sorrows into glee
No, I'm that kind,
I'm selfish..
I'm doing this because I like your smile..

46. From a hopeless romantic

I'm a hopeless romantic
Crazy dreamer, and a lover
I keep jumping from insane heights,
In a hope that you'll catch me at the fall
Reciprocating all the love I give
Listening to your heartbeat
In the rhythm of my poems
Feeling the warmth of your breath
As you exhale your love on my cheeks
It's hard to believe
We can have a forever together
But it's a beautiful dream
To which, I wish to surrender
It's easy to know when u fall in love
But it's hard to stay
And even harder to accept
The flaws, scars, and bitter truth your love comes with.
To love is easy and lazy
But to be in love needs strength and courage
So I live in hope, you'll accept me as a whole

We'll have this little eternity together
Even if there's no tomorrow
We'll live in this moment "forever"

47. Until we meet

Only if you were mine to keep
I would put my head on your shoulder and weep
About all those days...
And all those nights...
I spent without you...
Losing myself, just to find you...
If I could turn back time
I would make you mine
And I know that would be divine..
When it's cold outside
I would hug you tight
We'll cuddle throughout our ride
The morning adventures
And the long drives...
Beauty of nature
And you by my side
What else do I need
When your presence is my pride
I would rather stop the time, Only if I could
And stay with you, All the time
My hands in your pocket
N u holding them to keep me warm

SANJANA

My head on chest
And you caressing my back
Just to keep me calm
Only if you were mine to hold
Only if you were mine to keep
I would stay with you forever
Until the next time we meet

48. Happy that you exist

I thank god for your sheer existence....
This is how much I love you
Even when everyone is around
I still miss you
I wanna run to you
And never come back
I wanna stick with you
Through highs and low
I wanna shower on you happiness
And make a world of our own
You are sum total of all my wishes
You are the source of all my hopes and dreams
You are the return
Of every good deed, I ever did in my life
I need to tell you
How I feel, when your hands are holding mine
Soothing me, calming me, making me happier than ever before
You gave me
The warmth and love I craved for
And now, when you are there for me
And you promise to be with me
I wanna ask for something

Only if you wish to give me...
The next time we meet
Just Give me a hug
Just wait, hold on,
Hold me a little tighter
And for a bit longer
Hold my hand, just the way you do
Hold me, pull me back
Brush my hair aside
And whisper in my ears
That you love me...
And plant a forehead kiss
To assure me...
Yaa.. I can be needy sometimes
But you won't regret calling me "mine".

49. In most terrific times

Meeting you was like taking a breath of fresh air...
you reminded me of none, and that's fair..
You made my dreams come to reality,
you pulled me out of virtuality,
You made me believe I'm worth the love and care...
As for me, you were always there...
you knew how much I adore you...
and you left me in awe..
Even before I could know...
I couldn't let you go...
you promised to stay forever...
No matter what happens wherever...
I feel safe when you are around ..
In the most terrific time...
you became my fav sound...
you held together my scattered piece
And with you .... I'm always at peace...
I wish to look into Your deep eyes..
And there the time would freeze

50. Closer to closure

She is drifting apart
Because of the lies, he told
He is standing still
Hiding the tears he holds
Two souls who love each other unconditionally
Are now moving away....but only physically
Strings of their hearts are still connected
To behold the bond of love
Her mind has rejected
Their once cheerful conversation
Has now become a heated argument
They are challenging each other
And planning agreement
The final decision is yet to come
The one about which no one can ever think
Their hearts wanna come closer
But the mind has broken every link
The bitter truth..they will face
Moving apart ...they will still chase
The forehead craving for a kiss will get creases
The caressing heart will b torn into pieces
The idol couple for all others is fighting in the name of care

AMOUR

Going against their mind
Their hearts won't dare
The souls who wanted to get closer
Are now getting their bond's closure

51. Love has its dark side

She wasn't evil by birth at last
But it's due to what she faced in her past...
An innocent fairy turned into an evil witch
She gave back to the prince
In what her heart was rich
He was longing for love
She was filled with rage
Her beauty bounded him
And now, he was in a golden cage
Little did he knew
He was falling for a psycho
She kept building walls around them
Just to hear his pain ECHO
They lived in a dark place
Where nobody else could chase
He was tortured in the name of love
While she wore a sweet innocent face
Initially, with her name he blushed
Then soon , his love was crushed
From brightest red to darkest blue
On his scars...her fingers brushed
True love was laid bleeding

For mercy, his heart kept pleading
The bitter truth was now in front of his eyes
But SHE was as cold as ICE
His pretty sunshine
Couldn't stop her hurricane
Deep inside his brain
A loud gunshot came
He tried giving her, his love's crown
He only wanted to remove her heart's frown
But the leap of faith never worked...
And her evil shadow knocked him down

52. Little things

It's always the little things that matter
When we are in love..
The way your eyes shines
With your smile bright
When we hug each other tight..
The way we wish for the same things
In different ways
When we close our eyes…
The way we live for moments
To happen between us
When somehow they slip away
The way we wanna make love
Over and over again
Not the way they show in movies
But then we like it
Talking, holding hands, walking along the beachside
Letting the waves kiss our feet
While we kiss each other's souls
These are the things that matter
The way we remember small details
The way we want our memories to never fade
The way we want to love

AMOUR

The way we have each other's back
Devoting myself completely to you
Making you mine
The way it feels divine.

53. Have you ever been in love?

Have you ever really been in love?
It isn't that beautiful, as one portrays it to be
It isn't that easy either…
But then it's not even bad…
I mean.. common.. every coin has two sides.
It's scary, don't romanticize its power
But it's peaceful.. don't ruin its aura
It's not meant to be perfect..
Being in love is all about adjustments…
It takes time, compromise, and your whole damn heart
But in return, you get a lifetime of serenity…
It feels sane to be insane with the person you love
You can be annoying AF , still that person will adore you
Love is all about acceptance
Choosing to love the person for who they are
No complaints, no demands
It's about being selfless,
Everything you do is unconditional
Straight from heart,
No filters, no adulterations

AMOUR

Just pure like that.
But that's not it
With love comes pain
The pain of losing yourself in search of someone else
With love comes fear
Fear of not being enough
With love comes sacrifice
Sacrificing yourself for your better half
With love comes chaos
Chaos even in silence
With love comes us
Not just me, not just you
It's about us.. altogether

54. Was this a dream?

Were you there right next to me,
Or was I dreaming, being half-asleep??
Were you actually holding my hand,
Or was it just a sweet Imagination??
Were you speaking your heart out,
Or was I creating scenarios in my head again??
Were we there together for real, Or was I high ??
Were we loving each other,
Were we hugging each other,
Were we Kissing in the cold
Or is it just a dream I hold??
A dream too sweet
To turn into reality..
A dream too pure
To live in virtuality..
A dream so real
That I forgot reality !!
Is just me, dreaming all this,
Or do you feel the same??
Do you dream the same??
Do you wish the same??
Or is it just me going insane !!!

55. I dream a lot.

To lay on the grass green
With you by my side,
My soul screams
I wanna hold your hand
And speak my heart out
I wanna look at these shimmering stars
And hear you speak
I wanna look into your eyes
And peep into your soul
Neither asking why
Nor wanting more
Just you and me
Becoming us as whole
as you speak and voice reaches my heart
I measure the distance between heaven and earth
Just to realize, heaven is right beside me.
I promise you an eternity
Of unconditional love and care
To hurt your soul, I wouldn't dare
I wanna reach all your secret places
Touch your heart
Nourish your soul

And make you mine
I'm risking so much
Expecting you to do this to me
I love you deeply
Asking for nothing less
But always wanting more
Of you, of us ....

56. The moment I fell in love

When I fell in love with you
I lost my focus on the outer world
Yet my vision was crystal clear
Amidst this blurriness and chaos
Because I was looking at this world from your POV
The way I could never see
I looked at your two eyes
With four of mine
And I knew, this is gonna be divine
When I fell in love with you
I had no clue of what was happening
We were strangers until we had a fight
I apologized and your mood was light
We became friends and soon turned into best friends
From deep conversations to random shit
We Shared anything and everything
But when did I fall in love?
When you asked me to come out and play because I was sitting
alone?

When you taught me how to feed puppies, your eyes pooling with
love and care?
Or when you told me, everything will be alright
Because you'll always be there for me?
Or did it happen when I looked into your two sparkling eyes
With four of mine
Replaying all the little moments
And falling for you in every one of them…

57. When did you break the walls?

The walls I built around my heart
Was once suffocating
But now it's reallocating
It's a warm because place to stay
After you came in that day
Now I'm feeling at peace,
Now I'm rebuilding with pieces...
The pieces of my broken heart
That once tore us apart
Are now getting back in place
And you are my solace
I wanna hug you
And hold you for hours...
And let moment
Forever last !!!!

58. Being an old soul isn't easy.

I'm an old soul in this new world
A world full of hookups n no commitment
*I'm stuck with *Jaane Tu ya Jaane Na**
*And people are moving on with *Titliyan**
I'm a sunset person
The one who likes long walks
Deep conversations and holding hands
Stuck with people interested in a one-night stand
I would rather lay down under the dark sky
And talk about life n dreams
Then go to clubs, sipping vodka
Dancing and being mean
I'm born in the wrong generation
Where love has lost its meaning
Where people would rather breakup
Than fixing problems
There's no place for handwritten letters
In this world of Netflix and chill
So here I'm...
*Grumbling for my *Bechara Dil**

59. Someday..

Some day, you'll come
You'll come and you'll love
We would stay under the night sky
Singing silence, without asking why!!?
Why we fell apart... Why are we holding on...
Why weren't we together..
Why aren't we strangers anymore...
Why we can't be separated,
Why the mistakes we repeated,
Why can't we move away ..
Why are we still on the way...
Why do we love each other,
Why can't we still be lovers ..
Why are we still just friends
When we know, that's not how it ends...
Why can we sit in silence
How can we be at peace...
Why do we keep running away!!?
Why can't we fall apart?
Why are we still attached!!?
Why is it a perfect match !!??

60. Just you and me.

The only place I wanna be

Is the place with just you and me

Anywhere would feel like home

If you are there with me

I would take you to places

You have never seen

The place that doesn't exist in reality

We would travel in a world of own

Because with you, is my home

Just hold my hand

And run with me

Come to the heaven

Where resided just you and me

Hug me tight,

And stay the night,

Let's watch the stars shine

Ya, I know it's cold outside

Let's grab a blanket and cuddle inside

because of all the places, i wanna be

Is the place with just you and me.

61. Sometimes..

Sometimes in this lifetime
We meet a special soul
Someone, we can call our own
I met one such person in my high school
We have been friends since then
And now I'm in love with my best friend
And this feeling is nothing less than divine
He shares his life with me, and I share mine
Our life was never like a fairytale
Sometimes things were bright, and sometimes they were pale
With all the ups and downs, highs and lows
We kept nurturing our love, to help it glow
More than a relationship, what we have is a partnership
We are lovers with a strong friendship
In this strange plastic world
Our bond is holy and pure
To all the problems and issues
Togetherness is the only cure.

62. Not a suicide note

If one day, u see me dying...
Don't pretend to be sad . ...
I'm a long time dead...deep inside...
If one day, you hear about my death...
Don't mourn.....
because u didn't care enough when I was alive...
If one day you feel my poem
Don't praise its beauty...
They aren't your own..
If the one you see my picture..
Don't try to remember the happy moments we had..
because back then you were busy with something in your head
If one day you get this note..
Don't blame me for being on my own..
because you weren't interested to know
I belonged to which zone...
And if one day...you feel my pain..
Don't curse yourself.... you'll have no gain ...
As the drought would then be over ...
N there will be showers of rain....
And things won't be the same again....

63. Take me back to the night we met

Since the day you walked in
Even the stone-cold heart became warm
Since the day you held me,
I knew how happy I'll be evermore!!
I wish we could meet sometime,
When none of us would have to leave,
You would stay forever,
This is what my heart believes,
I wish you would hold me closer,
And fix me to the extent,
I won't ever be broken!!
I wish I could make you smile,
I wish I could call you mine,
I would walk a thousand mile
Only if you promise to stay by my side.
I hope when we meet again,
We would help each other get over every pain...
I hope when we meet the next time,
We wouldn't leave each other
Until the stars shine...

We would stay forever
We would go wherever
Where we could be together
Sitting under the night sky,
Under the same blanket and a hot mug of coffee
Our fingers dancing to the rhythm
Take me back to the night we met
Imagining if could love each other anymore,
Confessing the FEW THINGS left unsaid,
Feeling are emotions left unfelt
Hugging each other in the moonlight
Not leaving each other until the sunrise
Praising the beauty of the dark sky
Singing in peaceful silence
Looking at streets we walk by
Where I'll completely be yours,
N you would completely be mine

64. Why did I let you go?

Why did I let you go?
When I love you so much
I held you so close,
It was last summer...
We hugged and we kissed
The moments I missed
I had all I wanted
I forgot my past
Wanted these moments to last
Memories shadows that cast,
Why did I let you go..
Are we still near, Or are we drifting apart..
I made a mess
I wanna tear open my heart
To show you how much I love you
How much I miss you
And I still care for you..
I stumbled in my way
Lost you, my home
And now I'm feeling alone
Is it too late, To hope u didn't move on
I wanna hold you closer

I wanna make you mine
I promise to be wiser this time
I wanna spend my life
With you by my side
I wanna make it alright
I wish I knew this before
This is my love
And not folklore…

Let's fall in Love together..

www.ingramcontent.com/pod-product-compliance
Lightning Source LLC
Chambersburg PA
CBHW071918120726
48001CB00005B/1773